PORT TWILIGHT

Or

The History Of Science

A Chronicle of Folly, Wisdom, and Madness

Human life is brief, yet true knowledge is without end

Len Jenkin

BROADWAY PLAY PUBLISHING INC
224 E 62nd St, NY, NY 10065
www.broadwayplaypub.com
info@broadwayplaypub.com

First printing: May 2012
I S B N: 978-0-88145-526-7

Book design: Marie Donovan
Page make-up: Adobe Indesign
Typeface: Palatino
Printed and bound in the U S A

PORT TWILIGHT was first produced by the Undermain Theater in Dallas, Texas with the first performance on 5 November 2009. The cast and creative contributors were:

Josh Blann
Jonathan Brooks
Bruce DuBose
Jessica Cavanagh
Ariana Cook
Shannon Kearns-Simmons
Anastasia Munoz
Danielle Pickard
Ian Sinclair
Christian Taylor
Stefanie Tovar
Kent Williams

Director ....Katherine Owens
Set ....John Arnone
Music ....Bruce DuBose
Costumes ....Giva Taylor
Lights ....Steve Woods
Video ....Jeffrey Franks

DRAMATIS PERSONAE

MEN

DANIEL MILTON, *PhD in chemistry and molecular biology, post-doc work in genomics*
MARTY SCHOTT, *a B-movie producer/director*
DACK, *a phantom and an actor, with* DONNA
JERZY, *a local boy, and a jack of all trades*
RABBI, *a master of magical science*
MOSHIACH, *a messiah of the wrong kind*
SERVANT, *an orphan and a lover*
UNCLE NICK, *a vision in an apron*
MR CHANG, *a deskclerk*
MR ARGENTO, *an organ grinder*
TOMAS, *a monkey with a tin cup*

From the movie: Pleasantview 2100:
BOBBY BARLETT
PROFESSOR QUINE, *a scientist*

WOMEN

JULIETTE, *a student, with her share of trouble*
ABBY CHILDRESS, *a novelist turned screenwriter*
KIMMIE SCHOTT, MARTY'S *wife, a queen of the Bs*
DONNA, *a phantom and an actor*
CLINICIAN, *a tool of the Clinic*
RABBI'S DAUGHTER, *an addict*
O P M E STATION CHIEF, *a believer*

From the movie: Pleasantview 2100:
SUZY JOHNSON
BIG MABEL
DIANA DIAMOND

OTHER

SCIENTISTS IN A ROW, *watching and waitin*
ALIEN/SATAN/MR SOFTEE, *a changing face on a screen*

Progress might have been alright once, but it has gone on too long.
Ogden Nash

Somebody bring me some water
I'm burning up alive
Koko Taylor

1.

(On the outskirts of Port Twilight, a row of SCIENTISTS. *Near them, a hatrack. They look out toward the horizon. The men are in suits and fedoras, or white labcoats. The women are in businesslike suits or dresses, or white labcoats. A latecomer puts his fedora on the rack, joins the group. One of them checks a watch. They wait.)*

A SCIENTIST: *(Sings)* Enjoy yourself, its later than...

OTHER SCIENTISTS: Shhhhh!

(A red warning light begins to pulse on and off. A siren. They all put on dark glasses. They continue to look out. Darkness. The siren continues, fades. Silence)

2.

(In the distance, the wheezy music of an organ grinder. DACK sits at a desk, suit jacket over his chair. He smokes, checks over some papers. DONNA is nearby, black dress, doing her make-up, checking herself out in a full-length mirror.)

(DACK looks out at the audience.)

DACK: Here we are. I'm Dack. That's Donna. Donna! Say hello to the nice people.

DONNA: Hello. Welcome to Port Twilight.

DACK: We all know Port Twilight, don't we? The violet streetlamps along the boulevards, the endless grid of silent houses beyond the railroad line, Chinatown with its penny arcades and fan-tan parlours, rusted hulks of freighters in the harbor, the Wax Museum out on the Palace Pier, the dog track, the circus in its winter quarters near the White River, and the solitary fishermen along its muddy banks.

DONNA: Open-air cafes, moving walkways, flophouses, the motordrome. You remember. It's familiar, that tune...

(The organ grinder, MR ARGENTO, becomes visible. He's a hunchback with his monkey, TOMAS. TOMAS wears a cap, and carries a tin cup.)

DONNA: Mister Argento with his monkey Tomas, shaking his tin cup. They're always in front of the Clinic. Nearby, the Church of the Transfiguration with its great stone bell. One street over, the Twilight Ballroom. I'm the Hostess, but it's closed. Temporarily. For renovation. I've got other employment. So does Dack. Listeners.

DACK: At O P M E.

DONNA: And we're actors...

DACK: Sometimes. When there's nothing else that...

DONNA: We sing.

DACK: Dance. Whatever pays. We've got a few days on a movie, shooting in a warehouse on the outskirts, by the Autumn Park. Beyond the park, Raven Laboratories, the gigantic necropolis of Mount Endor Cemetery...

DONNA: ...and the limestone caves where Gypsies live. Beyond the caves, la selva oscura, the dark forest. Leopards.

DACK: Wolves. At this moment, a redtail hawk circles high above, looks down on Port Twilight with the indifference of a careless god.

(The organ grinder's music fades. In another space, JULIETTE appears, walking slowly.)

DONNA: There's Juliette.
She moved here with her boyfriend, from someplace in Minnesota...

DACK: Edena.

JULIETTE: Edina. Rhymes with mynah. Like the bird.

DONNA: Jimmy dumped her when he found out she was pregnant. Just disappeared.

JULIETTE: I hope he's back in Minnesota, goes ice fishing, falls through the hole, gets trapped under the ice, and needle-nose pike eat off his face.

DONNA: She had an abortion after he split. Took all the money she was saving up to go to art school. Pity. She works the 4-12 shift at Nick's Diner, busing tables.

(UNCLE NICK appears, a fat man in a chef's apron, with a moustache. He makes a crude gesture.)

DACK: That's the owner, Pop Tate. He grabbed her ass. She shoved him into the path of a waitress hauling three open face hot turkeys with gravy.

UNCLE NICK: Five ninety-five, with fries.

DACK: She's fired.

UNCLE NICK: I fire you!

JULIETTE: Go fuck yourself!

UNCLE NICK: Love...it hurts me.

He's gone. The organ grinder turns the crank again, a wheezy version of an aria from an Italian opera.

DACK: Now she's walking home to the Port Twilight Motel.

DONNA: Twenty bucks a night.

JULIETTE: Color T V. When its working.

DACK: A five mile walk. She's saving on carfare.

(*Organ grinder's music continues as* DACK *and* DONNA *head offstage.*)

DONNA: He always plays that same aria, from *La Forza del Destino*...

3.

(*A room in the Clinic appears. A female* CLINICIAN *in uniform. A single bed. Alongside it, a computer console. Hanging from the ceiling over the bed, like a steel chandelier, is the Tentacles, a device with eight arms. On each arm are electronic stimu-pads and auto-syringes. Along the arms are diodes that twinkle erratically. The Tentacles can lower and attach to a human body on the bed in one hundred places.*)

(*A pale young girl sits on the bed. This is the* RABBI'S DAUGHTER. *Through a curtained window, light from the street outside.*)

RABBI'S DAUGHTER: How much longer?

CLINICIAN: Connect too often to the Tentacles, sweetheart, you overload the circuits, shut down inside—cortex, cerebellum, hippocampus, thalmus— like a string of lights, synapse by synapse, till blackout.

RABBI'S DAUGHTER: How much longer?

(*The* CLINICIAN *is silent. The* RABBI'S DAUGHTER *lies down on the bed and curls into a ball. She's crying, her body shaking. After a long moment, the* CLINICIAN *shrugs, moves to the computer console. The lights on the Tentacles flicker, then glow. It begins a slow descent toward the bed. The girl lies on her back, and arches her body up toward the machine as if it was a descending lover.*)

CLINICIAN: Welcome back to paradise.

(The shadow of the hunchback organ grinder passes by the curtained window as the scene fades...)

4.

(DACK and DONNA, as the large lobby window of the Ramona Hotel appears. On it, in large letters: O P M E.)

DONNA: The old Ramona Hotel, closed for the season. Lawnchairs lie rusting in a forecourt overgrown with weeds.

(DACK sets up a lawnchair that's been lying on its side, sits. He's got a six-pack of beer.)

(JULIETTE reappears in the distance, still walking through Port Twilight.)

DACK: Here she comes, wound up tighter than a cheap watch. No love, no money.

DONNA: Under the arch of trees over the road, by the harbor where bodies of drowned sailors float in the surf. There she goes. Dark streets lit here and there by kerosene lanterns. Little kiosks on wheels selling souvenirs, homemade health tonics, pornographic and philosophical pamphlets.

(JULIETTE approaches, tries to peer inside the hotel.)

DACK: Hey! That's private. A very private...

DONNA: Research institute.

Donna walks over carrying a pizza box.

JULIETTE: Sorry. I was curious about O P M E.

DONNA: Off Planet Message Exchange.

JULIETTE: Off what?

DACK: Get your cute little ass out of here. We have work to do.

Juliette is gone. Lights dim as the outside wall of the
O.P.M.E. becomes an inside wall...

DACK: Of course, its too dim now, in this part of the
street, to make out more detail—the sign that reads
"Closed For Renovation," or the torn menu in the
gutter from a restaurant called Big Wong's, or the star
charts, signal amplifiers, headsets...

*(Lights up on the interior of the Off Planet Message
Exchange. The room was once the lobby of the Ramona
Hotel: check-in desk, ratty sofas, rows of room keys. It's full
of hi-tech audio equipment. Overhead, a giant video screen.)*

*(MONITOR 1 [DACK] and MONITOR 2 [DONNA] get
seated, headsets around their necks. The STATION CHIEF, a
businesslike woman, fiddles with equipment. MONITOR 1
and MONITOR 2 start on their pizza and beers. The STATION
CHIEF addresses them.)*

STATION CHIEF: Monitor Orientation Part Seven.
OPME has recently acquired the very 750,000 watt
transmitter from radio KZAM near Ensenada that sent
the Wolfman out so strong they heard him howling on
the moon. A sonic-phase self-modulating antenna is
on the roof of this very hotel. We broadcast 24-7: "You
are not alone. Please contact us at earliest convenience
blah blah blah plus a few nude shots and a pathetic
sampling of human bullshit—Shakespeare's sonnets,
Analects of Cconfucius, Beethoven's Third, the White
Album, recipe for apple pie. We monitor 200 possible
reply frequencies in real time, jacked in to Arecibo, the
Very Large Array south of Socorro, and the Cybersonic
Ear orbiting in the Asteroid Belt.
We are the lost children, abandoned at the edge of the
sea, and we ceaselessly scan the crowd of oiled bodies,
searching for our parents. We have to find them, and
we will.

(STATION CHIEF *flips on the large video monitor above.
It begins to show an occasional flash of jumbled data. The
monitors put on headset rigs, concentrate. We hear a dim
hum on speakers, the inchoate babble of the universe.*)

STATION CHIEF: *(To herself)* Are they avoiding us, like
you step around dogshit in the street?

MONITOR 1: Hypothesis One.

MONITOR 2: They don't fucking exist.

MONITOR 1: Two.

STATION CHIEF: Who can say what will lure a vastly
superior alien race into dialogue? Scientific curiosity?
Conquest? Commercial opportunities? Altruism?
Love? Think about it. Stay alert. I'll be back to check
your logs. *(She exits.)*

MONITOR 1: Hypothesis Three. They live in a parallel
dimension...

MONITOR 2: ...and the transit system is lousy. The bus
shows up once every million years.

Monitor 1 takes out a vial and two syringes.

MONITOR 1: A mixture of Oxycontin and Tibetan herbs
in a living biologic base, some kind of raccoon genome.
I get it from the Tango Professor. At the Twilight
Ballroom.

(MONITOR 2 *tosses off her headset, stands, starts taking off
her shirt.*)

MONITOR 2: Are you bored with the outdated
paradigm of flesh and bone?

MONITOR 1: *(Looking at her)* Not yet.

(MONITOR 1 *takes off his headset, tosses it aside.* MONITOR
2 *tosses aside her shirt.*)

MONITOR 1: You know, I'm getting the idea you still
love me. You know just when I...

MONITOR 2: It's the scanners mounted in my skull.
They read your iris volume, skin temperature, blood
flow. I adjust.

(MONITOR 2 *throws herself on* MONITOR 1. *As they tear
at their clothes, the hum from the audio devices grows
louder, and we can hear an occasional intelligible word, in
Chinese, French, Hindi, then gutturals as if some animal is
talking. On the video screen sets of random numbers flash
for a millisecond. Numbers above, sex on the couch below.
Darkness, and the O P M E office is gone.*)

5.

(*A row of violet streetlamps, extending off into the distance.
The* RABBI *stands alongside his tray of amulets for sale. He
wears a black hat and a black vest, under which we can see
the ends of his prayer shawl. His beard is white. Nearby
stands his* SERVANT, *a young man with a large old book, a
bottle of whiskey, and a shovel.*)

(JULIETTE *walks slowly past them.*)

SERVANT: Even now, after the sun has set, the heat in
Port Twilight is stifling. On the far side of the avenue
where Juliette walks, two men stand by a tray of
amulets for sale.

RABBI: (*Holding up different amulets*) Bring love to your
cold bed. Ward off the ayin ha'ra. Evil eye. Keep the
Black Wind away from your door.

SERVANT: The young man carries a shovel and a book.
(*He shows them.*) The "Genetic book of the Dead." The
old man lights a cigarette. The flame of the match
reveals his gray beard, stained yellow by nicotine near
his mouth. The young man with the shovel stares after
Juliette. She reminds him of someone... She disappears
at the far end of the avenue, in the shadow of the giant
cypress trees.

(JULIETTE *is gone. A distant sound of church bells. The* RABBI *closes his tray of amulets.*)

RABBI: I sold nothing. Not one amulet. The desperate citizens of Port Twilight no longer believe in the Holy Names. They'll starve me to death. No matter. After tonight, all will be changed. The end of days will be upon us, and the old world will fall away.

(The RABBI *hands the* SERVANT *the tray of amulets.)*

RABBI: Take this.

SERVANT: Yes, Rabbi.

RABBI: It's time. *(He starts walking.)*

SERVANT: Rabbi, where are you going?

RABBI: The White River.

SERVANT: On we go, past the dog track and the poolrooms, the endless grid of silent houses beyond the railroad line, blue glow of T V in the windows... The rabbi's not well. I carry his shovel to bury him wherever he may fall.

(The RABBI *stops, holds out his hand.)*

SERVANT: And his Johnny Walker.

(The SERVANT *hands the bottle to the* RABBI.*)*

RABBI: Black label. Heats the blood.

(The RABBI *takes a swig, wipes his mouth on his sleeve, hands it back to the* SERVANT.*)*

RABBI: Can you hear it? The river...

SERVANT: Yes, Rabbi. *(Pointing)* That way.

(The RABBI *walks. The* SERVANT *follows.)*

SERVANT: I have lived in the Rabbi's House of Study since I was two months old. Someone left me by the door in a green plastic garbage bag. He took me inside. On my fifth birthday I learned to sweep the room and

make tea for the old men who study the scrolls of the law. After work, I would play hide and seek with the Rabbi's daughter, a girl my own age.
I still sweep and make the tea. I am nothing—an orphan and a servant.

RABBI: Be quiet, for God's sake.

SERVANT: *(Softer)* On we go, past the penny arcades, fan-tan parlours, the circus in its winter quarters. A crescent moon. A half-dead fish lies gasping on the muddy bank of the White River.

(The RABBI *stops walking.)*

RABBI: Out of water will he be born...

(The RABBI *mumbles under his breath in Hebrew, rocking slowly back and forth. The* SERVANT *stands off to one side, looks steadily at the* RABBI, *his expression unreadable...)*

6.

DACK: Suddenly the setting changes. It's the Port Twilight Motel, sickly banana palms, a wishing well. A rooster pecks at an anthill between two flagstones.

*(*DANIEL MILTON *appears in his room at the Port Twilight. He is drinking Johnny Walker from the pint. He takes another hit, drags out a medical cooler. He pops it, and cold air comes out in a visible puff. He begins dumping the contents of the cooler—sealed test tubes, petrie dishes—into a large metal trash can he's dragged into the center of his room.)*

*(*DANIEL *holds one petrie dish up to the light, reads the label.)*

DANIEL: Jesus. I didn't even know we were working on this. This is evil shit. It ain't airborne, however. *(He tosses it into the trash can.)*

(In another space, DACK *and* DONNA, *a desk and a mirror.)*

DACK: Daniel Milton has been employed at Raven Laboratories, on the outskirts of town. Until today. He got a bit angry at the director...

DANIEL: Fuckin' A.

DACK: ...about what the lab was doing, pissed about the lies they told him. He threw some expensive glassware against a wall.

DONNA: They fired him.

DANIEL: I quit.

DACK: Kicked his ass out of there.

DANIEL: Calling me fucking presumptuous to question lab policy...

DONNA: On his way out, Danny boy used his passkey for the last time, scooped into a cooler all the viral agents developed over the past two years, along with the hard drive of his computer with all relevant data, threw it into his trunk, and headed back to the Port Twilight Motel.

DACK: Twenty bucks a nite. He's broke. Alimony.

DONNA: Child support. Bad luck.

DANIEL: The salient fact is there were enough nasty cultures up there to pretty well turn three or four states into graveyards. Dawn of the dead, in spades.

DONNA: Mister Big Shot. Johnny Come Lately With a Conscience. They'll blackball him from working as a molecular chemist, any lab, anywhere.

DANIEL: Maybe the Sudan, make mustard gas to kill black babies...

DACK: They'll also sue him, and throw his ass in jail.

DONNA: If they catch him.

DANIEL: Never will. I'm gonna be a mountain man. In the blue Canadian Rockies. Self sufficient. Leave this modern world in the dust. But before I pick up a Bowie knife and a strong woman to tan hides, I gotta finish the job here...and get some cash money.

(DANIEL *keeps drinking Johnny Walker, keeps smashing the petrie dishes into the trash can. He hauls some Clorox bottles out of a closet. He pours a bottle of Clorox into the trash can, then staggers, drunk, crashes to the floor, hits his head. Blood. He moans.)*

7.

(The front counter of the Port Twilight Motel. JULIETTE *appears. So does* MR CHANG, *an elderly deskclerk.)*

DONNA: Juliette's come home. You remember the Port Twilight Motel—the sickly banana palms, the wishing well with its rotting signboard...

JULIETTE: *(Reading)* "Drop a penny in the well, make a wish and never tell."

*(*MR CHANG *reads the Racing Form, drinks Johnny Walker from a highball glass.)*

JULIETTE: Evening, Mister Chang.

MR CHANG: Miss Juliette. You owe rent.

JULIETTE: I got fired. I have no money.

MR CHANG: Unfortunate. This may lead to unpleasantness.

JULIETTE: It's a fucking major problem, Mister Chang.

MR CHANG: It often is.

(A loud groan from off, then a crash.)

MR CHANG: Ah. Your neighbor in room 7 is drinking again. Goodnight, Juliette. *(He returns to his Racing Form.)*

(Back to DANIEL's room. He lies there motionless near the trash can. His head is bleeding. JULIETTE comes in the open door.)

JULIETTE: Hey, Mister Milton! Hey! You O K? I don't mean to intrude, but...

(JULIETTE kneels down by DANIEL's body, shakes him.)

JULIETTE: Wake up! Wake up!

(DANIEL stirs, groans, touches his head. He sees his own blood on his hand.)

DANIEL: I'm dying!

JULIETTE: Its only a cut.

DANIEL: I know you. You're the angel of mercy, come down to heal me...

JULIETTE: Sure I am. That's me, angel of mercy.

DANIEL: 'Scuse me, angel. Gotta finish this job. *(He manages to stand, throws another laptop computer into the trash can.)* Hard drives. Two years work. *(He pours in a bottle of Clorox.)* Clorox. Kills anything, even at supermarket strength. *(He rips down a curtainrod, stirs the Clorox/petrie dish/hard drive mixture with it.)*

JULIETTE: That stuff stinks.

DANIEL: You noticed.

JULIETTE: What the fuck are you doing? You know, Mister Chang is gonna kick you outta here.

DANIEL: Oooh, I'm shaking.

(The phone rings. DANIEL ignores it, keeps stirring. Finally, JULIETTE picks it up.)

JULIETTE: *(On phone)* Hello? *(She listens, and then, with one hand over the receiver...)* Some man wants Doctor Milton.

DANIEL: That's me.

8.

(Near the White River. The RABBI and his SERVANT carrying the shovel, the amulets, the whiskey, and the "Genetic Book of the Dead.")

RABBI: Still, we suffer. Fire and flood. Hunger. Disease. War. Old age and death. The Messiah--Moshiach—has not come.
In the stinking cellar of a bar in Zydas Street a manuscript was buried by the last Vilna rabbi, the holy Rabbi Pincus, before the Nazis killed him in '42. It was brought to Port Twilight. Worms had eaten holes in the pages, yet it revealed the sacred words to call Moshiach to us. *The Genetic Book of the Dead...*

SERVANT: An undecipherable mess of Yiddish, Hebrew...

RABBI: Moshiach's D N A is unchanged since the beginning of time. D N A in amber. Without chromosomes. Blank. He can become anything.

SERVANT: Listen to me, Rabbi...

RABBI: Moshiach will be born out of the river, like Moses.

SERVANT: Rabbi, either you're a fool, or you're a lunatic. God has abandoned this world. No holy words will bring Moshiach and lead us back to Eden.

RABBI: Ungrateful motherless bastard. Be silent, do what I instruct you. You know nothing abo...

SERVANT: Your House of Study is a refuge for homeless men. They piss in the corner by the stove. You can't pay me. Do you ever wonder why I still serve you?

RABBI: I let you sleep in the cellar. I...

SERVANT: For your daughter's sake.

RABBI: My daughter is dead.

SERVANT: You lie to me, Rabbi. A good man wouldn't lie to me. Not even in Port Twilight.

RABBI: She's dead. Two years now.

SERVANT: I love her. I loved her since we were five years old. She's disappeared. I search, night after night, wandering these streets. You must know where she is. I beg you to tell me.

RABBI: Our father Abraham had the essence of the 22 letters burned onto his tongue. Then he spit them out among the seven stars. Give me the book, and bring me to the river.

9.

(Back to DANIEL*'s motel room. He is on the phone, listening.* JULIETTE *sprawls in a chair. In another area nearby,* DACK *and* DONNA*.)*

DONNA: Who's on the line?

DACK: Marty. Marty Schott, the producer hyphen director, King of the Bs. The tits and ass schlockmeister. Old college buddy of Daniel's. He's shooting a film in Port Twilight.

*(*MARTY SCHOTT *appears in another space, the film set/ warehouse, on the phone with* DANIEL*. The warehouse is only dimly lit behind him.* KIMMIE SCHOTT *is nearby.)*

MARTY: *(On phone)* They want to get out of the adult room at the videostore and into the mall but keep it sexy and simple so they can still sell to Chinese T V and Telemundo...

DACK: This time Marty's German backers have fronted him real money.

DONNA: Hans and Fritz need some class--they were almost jailed last month for tax evasion.

MARTY: Here's the kicker. Hans and Fritz want me to set it in the future. 2100. Science fiction. Sexy science-fiction. I built this spaceship in the warehouse, Danny. Dream cast, but the script is fucked. Schedule says I start shooting tomorrow and its fucked. I hired Abby Childress, for God's sake.

DANIEL: *(On phone)* Who's Abby Ch...

MARTY: *(On phone)* Smart as hell, she can write, but her idea of the future looks like a Jetsons outtake. Talk to my writer, Danny.

DANIEL: I don't think I'm...

MARTY: I saw that T V thing you did about the future of the planet, for God's sake. I even taped it. "Scientists Look at Tomorrow."

DANIEL: No.

MARTY: Five thousand a week, long as it takes. Danny, my balls are in the fire here...

DANIEL: I never even go to the movies...

MARTY: You don't have to make the damn thing. You're only the Futuristic Consultant. As they say, it ain't rocket science.

DANIEL: I could use the money. My lab just...

MARTY: Beautiful. A car'll be there in twenty minutes. Bar in back, Tanqueray and tonic. Limes.

DANIEL: Who's starring in this one?

MARTY: Kimmie. Who else?

DANIEL: Like old times.

Daniel looks over at Juliette. She waves.

DANIEL: I'm gonna need my research assistant. Invaluable girl.

MARTY: You banging her?

DANIEL: She's my post-doc in computational genomics.

MARTY: What's she gonna cost me?

DANIEL: *(To* JULIETTE, *hand over phone)* What are you making at Hooter's?

JULIETTE: It isn't Hooter's. It's Tate's.

DANIEL: How much?

JULIETTE: They fired me.

DANIEL: *(To* MARTY *on phone)* A thousand a week.

MARTY: You're robbing me, Danny. Just get your ass over here.

*(*MARTY *hangs up.* JERZY, *in the distance, takes out his tin whistle, plays a quiet tune.)*

MARTY: He's coming, Kimmie. He'll be here.

DONNA: Kimmie's been the star of every one of Marty's movies, ever since *Zombie Island*. He found her at an auto show. She was sitting on the hood of a Chevy Malibu in a bikini. He liked her right away.

KIMMIE: Danny's not doing so well since the divorce. Shot his mouth off at some genetics conference, blaming the scientific establishment for something or other. It even made the papers.

MARTY: He's still a fucking genius. Well? Isn't he?

KIMMIE: So they say. Probably drinking too much.

MARTY: Don't we all. Jerzy!

(JERZY *sticks his tin whistle in his pocket, comes over.*)

JERZY: Yeah?

MARTY: I got a pick up for you.

JERZY: Port Twilight Motel, room 7.

KIMMIE: Kid hears everything.

MARTY: Take the Lincoln.

Marty tosses Jerzy car keys, and he turns to go.

KIMMIE: Jerzy! Don't drive that thing like it's your personal rocketship.

(JERZY's *gone.*)

10.

(MARTY *and* KIMMIE *and the film set/warehouse are gone.* DANIEL's *motel room.*)

JULIETTE: I didn't know you were a doctor.

DANIEL: PhD. I'm a molecular chemist, whatever that is.

JULIETTE: Look, Doctor, I gotta meet someone.

DANIEL: Who?

JULIETTE: What are you, my father?

DANIEL: You saved my life. I should watch out for you. And I'm curious.

JULIETTE: Pablo. He wants to take me out to eat.

DANIEL: Pablo is the fucking janitor. He's got a bad moustache.

JULIETTE: It's his payday.

DANIEL: He's a notorious substance abuser.

JULIETTE: I'm hungry.

DANIEL: He's short. Maybe five two.

JULIETTE: He was going to college in Guadalajara...

DANIEL: Sixth grade, sweetheart. Pack. For a couple weeks.

JULIETTE: Where am I going?

DANIEL: Vegas. We're putting it all on black.

JULIETTE: Red.

DANIEL: You're employed. I got you a lucrative position in the movie business.

JULIETTE: What do I have to do?

DANIEL: Make sure I don't hit my head again. A thousand a week. No joke.

(JERZY *appears, with the Lincoln. He stares at* JULIETTE.)

JERZY: You are so beautiful. You...

JULIETTE: Fuck this.

DANIEL: *(To* JULIETTE*)* Get in.

(JULIETTE *hesitates a long moment. She gets in.*)

DANIEL: *(To* JERZY*)* Kid, just drive.

(The three of them, in the Lincoln, driving. Uncomfortable silence)

JULIETTE: *(To* DANIEL*)* Where we going?

DANIEL: Somewhere. I didn't ask.

JERZY: To the warehouse, Miss. Where we make the cinema.
I'm Jerzy.

JULIETTE: Like the turnpike?

JERZY: Funny. Ha ha. Jerzy with a Z. I'm an actor.

DANIEL: Crank up the A C in here, Jerzy with a Z. It's hot as hell.

JERZY: The A C's dead. Has been for months.

DANIEL: Lovely.

JERZY: You new here, Miss?

JULIETTE: I got here a few months ago.

JERZY: I was born in Port Twilight. You want the history? Comes free with the ride.

JULIETTE: Just the highlights.

DANIEL: Don't encourage...

JERZY: This place was the heart of the great trade route. Iron tools, lenses, and Jesus from the West, fireworks, silk, and cinnamon from the East. Every courtyard stunk of camel dung.... *(He keeps talking on under, but we only hear fragments...)*

JERZY: ...black plague...crusades...fire...

(In their own space, DACK and DONNA.)

DACK: Jerzy said he's an actor. That's not exactly...

DONNA: Its bullshit. Jerzy is a local kid Marty picked up cheap. He makes the lunches, drives Marty and Kimmie around...

JERZY: You two married?

DANIEL: Newlyweds.

JULIETTE: We're neighbors.

JERZY: Sit back. Enjoy the ride in my Lincoln Towncar.

JULIETTE: Now that I'm riding in this towncar with you and all, can I ask you something?

DANIEL: Anything.

JULIETTE: Why do you live in the motel, when you have a real job? I see you go to work in the morning.

DANIEL: Alimony, child support. Bad luck. And it suits me. Neighbors are even more fucked up than I am. Not including you, of course.

JULIETTE: Of course. And what were you doing with that trash can? And the Clorox?

DANIEL: Oh, that. Top secret.

JERZY: We're here.

(The interior of the warehouse, once a fortune cookie factory, appears. All the baking machines are gone. Perhaps a stray sign in Chinese. Built inside the warehouse is a hi-tech set of a future spaceship interior—steel panels, cold white neon. A futuristic look, with flair. Off the set itself, work tables, chairs, computers, lighting equipment.)

(In an upstage corner, almost invisible, an old CHINESE WOMAN sits silently. She tucks fortunes into cookies, one by one.)

11.

(The Off Planet Message Exchange, though the spaceship set remains dimly visible. MONITOR 1 and MONITOR 2, with beer, cold pizza, and hi-tech equipment. They have headsets, and are plugged in. The giant T V screen flashes numbers in series, letters strung out to spell nothing, all too quick for the eye to catch. Unintelligible rumble and hiss from speakers, punctuated by static.)

MONITOR 2: Psychotic babble.

MONITOR 1: The psychotic babble of the spheres, a buzz laid down millenia ago in somefuck language in some other star system...

MONITOR 2: All conveniently filtered and descrambled by our state of the art decoding software that can't tell shit from Shinola, Sir Thomas Browne from Teen Suck Sluts, twenty gazillion times a milli-second.

Only thing out there is the Black Wind.

(Change in speaker sound to a kind of erratic gurgling.)

MONITOR 1: The waiting room for transit between
worlds never changes. Dust on the benches. Shoeshine
boy in the corner snaps his rag in the same rhythm for
ten million years...
You know what? I just remembered this story I read
once in a comic book. It was called "Pleasantview
2100!" Earth is doomed, I forget why, but they got this
one spaceship to save the human race...

*(Lights up on the spaceship set. A low hum. A giant clock.
DACK [MONITOR 1] becomes more melodramatic.)*

DACK: The U S S Clinton sails through the vast reaches
between the stars, silent as a tomb, except for the
hum of one hundred Permafrost Units, each a six foot
cylinder of clear plastoid, within which lies a human
body, skin blue with cold. Earth's last best hope—fifty
men and fifty women, chosen for their brains, and their
beauty. The clock on the bridge reads two years and
one day—the beginning of year three of a five hundred
year voyage.

*(BOBBY BARTLETT, in a 2100 space outfit, appears stealthily.
He slides a plastoid freeze unit out of a wall. On its side, the
name "Suzy Johnson".)*

DACK: All the meticulous psycho-testing never
revealed the depths of lust in Bobby Bartlett,
Lieutenant Junior Grade. He'd planned it all. And
now, as he leans over the voluptuous body of Suzy
JohnsonBetty Cooper, a slutty smile on her frozen face,
he recalls Professor Quine speaking to all one hundred
of them in the briefing room...

PROFESSOR QUINE: *(In BOBBY's mind)* You have been
chosen to make the five hundred year long journey
to the distant star Alcibiades. Circling that star is a

planet that can be terraformed—a new Eden. Our
Permafrost Units freeze the human body to extremely
low temperatures, keeping it in a state of suspended
development. Over those five hunded years, you
will not age a day. At the destination you will be
automatically thawed to....

DACK: Bobby was the tech in charge of the freeze pods.
So easy to reset the timing relays to thaw himself early.
Very early.

BOBBY: Fifty babes. All hotties! And I have my pick.

(BOBBYe *flips a switch on* SUZY's *Permafrost Unit. It makes
a thawing sound. Lights fade on the unit as he checks his
watch, strolls over to the bridge in front of the giant clock.)*

BOBBY: Let's see. I'm twenty-six now. Say I live to be
seventy-six. That would be one woman a year, not
even enough time to get tired of her. Man o man!

(SUZY JOHNSON, *blonde, stumbles onto the bridge, freshly
thawed.)*

BOBBY: Suzy!

SUZY: Bobby!

BOBBY: You're thawed out! Your relay must have
failed, like mine!

PROFESSOR QUINE: *(In their minds)* The human body can
stand only one freeze and one thaw. If you thaw early,
you'll live out your entire life on the U S S Clinton.

SUZY: Oh, Bobby. We have to live out our entire lives
on this stupid spaceship!

BOBBY: At least there's two of us, Suzy.

SUZY: I'm frightened. Hold me, Bobby! Kiss me...

BOBBY: Suzy baby....

DACK: They were alone on their spaceship island, alone and uninhibited. But after a few months, familiarity bred contempt.

(BOBBY *draws a paralyzer ray.*)

SUZY: Bobbykins! Why are you holding that paralyzer ray?

BOBBY: Suzy, I'm sick of your bubbleheaded remarks. I'm sick of that mole on your left breast.

SUZY: It's on the right...

BOBBY: We're finished.

SUZY: Omigod! I get it! You thawed me on purpose. You only wanted pussy!

BOBBY: That's right, Suzy. Once you're dead, I'll thaw one of the others. Till I grow old and senile, I'll taste fresh love.

(BOBBY *fires, paralyzing* SUZY. BIG MABEL *enters with a paralyzer ray. She's got him covered.*)

BOBBY: Big Mabel!

BIG MABEL: You're not the only one who can reset relays, Bobby.

BOBBY: What are you holding?

BIG MABEL: It's a paralyzer, Bobbykins. Just for you.

BOBBY: Mabel, you and me, we can be king and queen, make the rest of them slaves! We can...

BIG MABEL: I'll be queen all right. The Queen Bee. So long, Bobby! I never liked you anyway...

BOBBY: No, Big Mabel! I'm the only man left. I killed all the others!

BIG MABEL: (*Laughs*) You saved me the trouble. You see, Archie, I'm a lesbian. A very happy lesbian... (*She fires, paralyzing* BOBBY.)

BIG MABEL: *(To herself)* Now to thaw Diana! She'll be my first...

*(*DIANA DIAMOND, *brunette, comes in with a paralyzer ray.)*

BIG MABEL: Diana? I didn't thaw you yet. How...

DIANA: You're not the only one who can reset relays, Big Mabel. I'll have fifty boytoys, one by one. I've killed all the other women. Except you.

BIG MABEL: But then ev...

*(*DIANA *fires, paralyzing* BIG MABEL.*)*

DACK: Big Mabel was trying to say that all the men were dead too. Bobby killed them.
Four hundred forty-seven years to go. Diana Diamond sits alone on the bridge of the U S S Clinton. Her hair is white, and she looks out at an endless field of unfamiliar stars. Corpses rot in their Permafrost Units. She imagines her own skeleton, sitting in that same chair, the joker under her beautiful skin.
After a journey of five hundred years, the spaceship lands, and a great cloud of seeds is blown into the atmosphere--laurel, oak, pine--as the new planet is automatically terraformed for habitation by the dead.

12.

*(*DACK *is gone.* DIANA *holds a moment, then steps forward.)*

DIANA: That's it. The end. You need me anymore right now?

MARTY: Fucking unbelievable crap!

DIANA: I guess that means no.

*(*DIANA's *gone. In the warehouse, on the film set.* ABBY, DANIEL, JERZY, JULIETTE, KIMMIE *and* MARTY *have been watching this rehearsal.)*

MARTY: They're gonna kill us. They're gonna take away my house. My kids'll be out on the street.

ABBY: Marty, you don't have any kids.

MARTY: Kimmie's insides are a mess. Is that my fault?

KIMMIE: Marty, shut up.

MARTY: Kimmie, just tell me, am I right on this?

KIMMIE: On the money. The sex is sophomoric. It's got the same idea of the future as a Star Trek re-run. I'm sorry, Abby, but no one will pay to make this. When they see the script, or the first dailies, they'll pull the financing.

MARTY: Hans and Fritz fronted me more real mazola than they ever put down for anything. I spent a shitload of it on you and your script. I promised them a new vision of the future—two jumps ahead of the Harvard development sluts. They're gonna sue me. And then I'm gonna sue you. We have a contract. You took my money to deliver class. You delivered crap.

ABBY: I delivered a satiric look at science fiction and sex films. You don't seem to like it.

JULIETTE: It was funny.

DANIEL: My assistant. Postdoc in genomics.

MARTY: You don't get it, Abby. They are already moving the furniture out of my office, including the Italian credenza. You think I'm getting another shot after this? And after "Revelations?"

ABBY: "Revelations" was the best thing on screen last year. It's why I took this job. Kimmie should've gotten an Oscar.

KIMMIE: It lost money.

MARTY: Flatter us all you want. I'm still gonna sue your ass. The future is not sociopathic Bobby and Suzy bonking on a rocket.

ABBY: What is it then?

MARTY: How should I know?

DANIEL: That's not the future. That's the future in the movies, and that's all anybody knows, even if they're a decent novelist.

ABBY: Who the hell is he?

MARTY: Abby Childress, Daniel Milton, PhD. My pet futurist.

ABBY: You read a book of mine?

DANIEL: I don't have that kind of time. I googled you.

MARTY: That's my fancy writer, Danny.

DANIEL: I see her.

MARTY: She's trying to ruin me.
Your students at Brown would be ashamed. Abby, you're kicking me into the gutter, a forty-nine year old man.

KIMMIE: Fifty-five.

MARTY: I'll work the on-ramp selling oranges. This thing is supposed to start shooting tomorrow. I'm captain of the Death Star. This movie is my death star. Look, Danny, get rid of Bobby and Diana. Give me a future in the future, not a future in the past.

(DANIEL *takes a drink.*)

DANIEL: Might not be pretty.

KIMMIE: We'll take that chance.

(*Long beat*)

JULIETTE: Where did the other actors go?

KIMMIE: Dack and Donna? I got them rooms near the Old Market, over a karioke lounge. They're probably singing Delaney and Bonnie's greatest hits.

(DACK *and* DONNA *in another space. the song is Delaney and Bonnie's* Neverending Love.*)*

DACK & DONNA: *(Sing)*
I've got a neverending love for you
From now on, that's all I wanna do
From the first time we met I knew...

(Their song mixes with the RABBI*'s chant, then fades as we cross to...)*

13.

(The RABBI *chanting a prayer by the river. The* SERVANT *leans on his shovel.)*

RABBI: *(Chanting)*
Aleph, Ham, Shem
Three Holy Mothers,
Aleph, Ham, Shem,
Three Holy Fathers
Above the dragon Thele
Below the Third World
Shadow of the world to come...
(And repeating on under)

SERVANT: The Rabbi's lost it. I even feel sorry for him—believing his own bullshit, trying to open the lock of time, bring Moshiach into this world.

RABBI: Now Moshiach walks the nineteenth path, the Wheel of Ezekial. Now Moshiach walks the twelfth path, the Transparency. Now, out of water, while the crop is fat in the field, and King Harvest has not yet come. Moshiach! Moshiach! Moshiach!

(The RABBI *staggers, raises his arms high. A strange sound, as the fabric of space-time rips. And* MOSHIACH *rises from the water, a naked young man, dripping wet.)*

SERVANT: Holy shit!

(The RABBI *bows to* MOSHIACH, *then approaches him and hangs an amulet around his neck.)*

RABBI: My gift—to protect you.

(The MOSHIACH *speaks with a touch of guttural rasp in his voice.)*

MOSHIACH: You brought me here before my appointed time. Was this wise?

RABBI: Who can say what is wise?
Give him the clothing.

(The SERVANT *holds up a tuxedo on a hanger.)*

SERVANT: All I had. From my senior prom.

RABBI: Put it on, my Moshiach. Put it on.

*(*MOSHIACH *does so.)*

MOSHIACH: This place stinks.

RABBI: You are in Port Twilight, not a perfumed fairyland.

MOSHIACH: It smells like river mud and human shit.

RABBI: Listen to me, my Moshiach. Yeshua of Nazareth came and went. Men still slaughtered each other till the fields ran with blood, and Black Plague came and ruled the earth. Rabbi Nachman of Bratslav came and went. Children still died at the end of the bayonet and bombs turned cities into burning hells. Now you have come. Even here in Port Twilight, I have hope.
My science of the Holy Names of God is ancient and pure. The Baal Shem himself could not call you. Not even Rabbi Pincus, with his spiral alphabet... *(He grows*

short of breath. He takes a swig of whiskey, wipes his mouth on his sleeve.) Follow me.

(They walk through the Port Twilight night in a line, the RABBI, MOSHIACH, *and the* SERVANT. MOSHIACH *looks up, and stops walking.)*

MOSHIACH: Up above. The little lights...?

SERVANT: Those are stars. Far away. The big light is the moon.

MOSHIACH: How long will I live here to see such things? Stars...

SERVANT: I don't know.
There are things more beautiful than stars.

MOSHIACH: What? What things? Tell me.

SERVANT: Women. Certain women. Storms. Music.

MOSHIACH: I want them.

(On they walk. The exterior of the Clinic appears, with its small curtained window. In the distance, MR ARGENTO *the organ grinder and his monkey. The* RABBI *stops walking, turns to* MOSHIACH.*)*

RABBI: I don't have a congregation to worship you. The House of Study is in a stripmall, between a nail salon and a donut shop.

MOSHIACH: I need to feed. To sleep.

RABBI: You will sleep on the floor. You will eat black bread and drink tea. And there will be work for you. Not yet. You're not ready yet. *(To* SERVANT*)* I thank you. You didn't run when he rose up from the river. Wait here. We'll talk. *(He turns to enter the Clinic...)*

14.

(The row of SCIENTISTS *in suits or labcoats, and sunglasses. Near them, the hatrack with two fedoras. In another space,* DACK *and* DONNA.*)*

DONNA: At this point in the drama, once the Rabbi has turned toward the Clinic, intending to go in and see his daughter, the familiar row of scientists appears—the labcoats, fedoras, sunglasses.

(Silence. The SCIENTISTS *wait. A red light washes over the group. It pulses on and off. A siren.* DACK *and* DONNA *put on dark glasses. Suddenly all scientists dance Science Dance One.)*

(An impossibly harsh blast of white light. All SCIENTISTS *freeze mid-dance, like shadows burned onto a wall. The hat rack bursts into flames. As the light fades, white ash begins to drift down from above. Blackout.)*

15.

(The warehouse with the spaceship set. JERZY *sweeps up.* ABBY, DANIEL, JULIETTE, KIMMIE *and* MARTY.*)*

DANIEL: We're never gonna see that *Pleasantview 2100* future—sexy space cadets, rocket ships, the cryogenic dream of eternal life. The real future is elsewhere: horrific overpopulation, viral plagues, prion disease, earthquakes, tsunamis, casual genocide, religious crusades, race wars, general fucking chaos before some entrepreneur paves the whole planet over for an intergalactic parking lot and what's left of us move on. Unless—unless a half-dozen scientific breakthroughs happen, and we can make the whole damn biosphere—bacteria up to human beings—start to work our way. If my hands were just a little tighter around Mother Nature's throat...

ABBY: Let me see if I've got this right. You actually believe you know better than Mother Nature or God or whoever's currently in charge just how to run the planet?

DANIEL: Yeah. I'd run it without so much pain and suffering, thank you. I'd run it without cancer. Without species extinction. And with enough groceries. If nature wants crops to fail, I'm saying No. Everybody's got a full belly, fewer wars. If Mother wants you to get aids, diabetes, black plague, I'm gonna say No.

ABBY: Your fucking arrogance is unbelievable. "Nature" is us, blood and bone. We are it, along with the roaches and the rivers. When we forget that simple fact is when we screw up. We need to learn more from the natural world, not less, harsh as it can seem. It makes sense that there's a forest fire once in a while, or a lion eats a zebra.

DANIEL: Not if you're the zebra.
You know, I got fired today. From my lab.

ABBY: Join the party. I'm about to get fired from this job. Because of you. You think they kept my teaching job open at Brown?

DANIEL: How the hell should I know?

ABBY: That was sarcasm. They didn't. They were pissed I'd left the department for what they thought was Hollywood. They never heard of Marty.

DANIEL: And you had?

ABBY: Yes, I had. He's made a few really fine movies in the middle of all the junk.

(MARTY *approaches them.*)

MARTY: See, Danny. A woman with taste, refinement, and balls. Just give her a few notions, a few...

DANIEL: Marty, listen to me. I need the money, but you've got the movie-type ideas. Why don't you just give the lady a few of...

MARTY: 'Cause this particular piece of cinema history is supposed to be half-decent. Your ideas will be a helluva lot more accurate than mine about how we're gonna be living in a hundred years. And Hans and Fritz will be thrilled I hired you. Scientific Consultant, PhD. Employed by the U S Government on top secret...

DANIEL: I quit.

ABBY: They fired him.

MARTY: Good. No professional conflicts.

ABBY: Forget it, Marty. He needs a bath and a shave. He stinks of...

JULIETTE: Clorox. Is what it is.

ABBY: I can't work with him.

KIMMIE: Yes you can. He's just as smart as you are, and he always behaves himself in the end.

DANIEL: Kimmie, how does Marty manage to keep you around?

KIMMIE: I'm just too lazy to go out looking.

MARTY: You'd be on the street without me, baby.

KIMMIE: Sure. I find the money, line produce, take my top off for the goddamn camera, and I'm still willing to sleep with you.

MARTY: Kimmie, I was just...

KIMMIE: Marty, shut up.

ABBY: All right, Doctor Milton. Just give me something to work with here, and go back to wherever you came from.

(DACK *and* DONNA *begin singing a Delaney and Bonnie medley, softly. They continue under the following...*)

DANIEL: I've got a theory...

ABBY: Brilliant!

DANIEL: You a Bible banger?

ABBY: You kidding?

DANIEL: Some Christians think a scientific theory is something you just make up. Drunk all night, wake up in some stranger's bed, wonder for a moment who she might be, light up a joint, and then you think of it— the theory. (*To group*) I've got a copy of myself in my pocket, just lookin' for a body.

JULIETTE: "Scuse me?

(DANIEL *reaches into his pocket, pulls out a matchbox. He tosses it to* JULIETTE.)

DANIEL: That's me in there, total brain scan, digitized down to the last pathetic memory, a cortical stack ready to jack into any spinal column, half-hour surgery to create the plug, right below the medulla. Short circuits the resident brain, and takes over. Two of me walking around downtown, only one looks just like somebody else. I'd pick up a cheap synthetic body for it but they never get the elbow joint right, or the sex. You want real meat you gotta go to the meat market-- right here in Port Twilight, down by the Palace Pier.

JULIETTE: It's just a matchbox.

DANIEL: Is it now?

She opens it, lights a match, blows it out.

JULIETTE: Yeah.

(DACK *and* DONNA*'s music grows louder, a track comes in under the vocals, and a dance sequence begins.* ABBY, DACK, DONNA, JERZY, JULIETTE, KIMMIE *and* MARTY.)

(As the dancers dance, DANIEL *keeps talking—to the audience now. He takes a small pill container out of his pocket, shakes it.)*

DANIEL: Something new from the drugstore. High-level EMPATH drug, *(Reading label)* Vasopressin, Dopamine, Acetylcarnitine, Cobra Venom Concentrate. Take sex—you do someone, you feel what you're feeling and you feel what they're feeling. The drug is in your saliva. Pass it on. A drop on the skin and they feel what you feel, which is what you feel and what they feel. Feedback loop is infinite, can't tell who's you and who's who till the drug wears off at dawn... Or take a dose and just sit quietly, look at a dead pine tree.

(The dance continues as, like a magician, DANIEL *pulls something else from another pocket. This small bottle is glowing. He holds it up.)*

DANIEL: Nanobots. Little bio-chemical switcheroos. Drink me! *(He drinks it down, tosses it aside, begins to dance himself.)* Few billion nanobots just took up residence in my brain capillaries. Whooo! Remember, folks, eyes don't see, fingers don't touch—the brain does it all. You don't experience diddley till the big boy gets the message. Johnny Nanobot gets in there, and he's intercepting, changing, inventing the message. Any damn way you want. You program the little fuckers. It's Virtual Reality from inside, a hundred percent equal to the so-called "real world" in resolution and believability. Be someone else and be somewhere else! You never know it's Johnny Nanobot, 'cause it's all there is. All and everything. You might burn out a few neurons, but what the hell. Hey, everybody gets theirs. Wonderful, wonderful world.

(The music stops suddenly, with the sound of a needle screeching across a record. The dancers continue dancing for a beat, then are still. Crossfade to...)

16.

(Outside the Clinic. In the distance, the organ grinder plays. The RABBI, *the* SERVANT, MOSHIACH *in his tuxedo, exactly as before. The* RABBI *has just turned to go toward the Clinic. His* SERVANT *stops him.)*

SERVANT: Rabbi, this is the Clinic. Only addicts who have given over their souls to the Tentacles are housed here. The lowest of the low. Even God has forgotten them. Why do...

RABBI: Who is to say who is high, and who is low? Maybe Moshiach knows. Ask him. I have to visit someone.

MOSHIACH: When will I sleep and dream my dreams? When will I feed?

RABBI: *(To* SERVANT*)* Watch him. Keep him close. *(He disappears inside the Clinic.)*

*(*MOSHIACH *stares up at the night sky.)*

SERVANT: Two men stand in the darkness outside the Port Twilight Clinic. The moon is high. The one in the tuxedo has the power to heal, to find what is...

MOSHIACH: *(Interrupting)* Tell me. About the lights.

SERVANT: That row of seven stars is the Aleph--the seven gateways of a man's body. Those stars are the dragon, Thele, who circles the world...

MOSHIACH: Tell me. About the storms, and the women.

(Their voices fade as the exterior wall of the Clinic becomes an interior wall. The SERVANT *and* MOSHIACH *are gone.)*

(The RABBI'S DAUGHTER *lies face-up on the bed. The Tentacles, lit and pulsing, hover just above her. Like an octopus-lover, it clings to her body at many points, either by stimu-pad or the point of a syringe. A thick mass of wires runs to her skull. The* CLINICIAN *sits at the computer*

console, making adjustments. The RABBI *stands in a corner, watching. He rocks slowly back and forth.)*

(The RABBI'S DAUGHTER'S *body writhes, strains upwards towards the machine. The* RABBI *prays.)*

RABBI: I will bring the prisoner out from the prison house. I will make darkness light before her, and crooked roads straight... These things will I do, and not forsake...

*(*RABBI'S DAUGHTER *moans in violent pleasure and/or in pain. It is impossible to tell. The* RABBI *falls to his knees.)*

RABBI: *(Mourner's Kaddish in Hebrew, softly)* Yisgadol v'yisgadash, shmay ra'aboh...*(and continuing...)*

(In another area, DONNA.*)*

DONNA: There's no point in going further with this scene, which everyone already knows—the impassive technician, the machine delivering its message of pain and pleasure, the Rabbi's body rocking as he prays. And the face of the Rabbi's daughter as she looks up at the Tentacles, her eyes glittering, hard and empty as diamonds.

17.

(The warehouse holding the spaceship film set, work tables, chairs. KIMMIE *and* MARTY, ABBY *and* DANIEL, JERZY *and* JULIETTE. JERZY *plays a tune on his tin whistle. There's a bottle of Johnny Walker. A story meeting, and a party of sorts.)*

ABBY: Try on this future. The computers get to where they are no longer designed by idiots, a.k.a. homo sap erectus, but are re-engineered by themselves, and the smarter they get the more they can make themselves smarter, and before we look around, we're not even service techs. We're pets. Woof! Woof! And this machine intelligence is a shark, with primordial programming to feed, grow, and reproduce. It does these things at the speed of light. To ask about its purpose once it's rolling is as pointless as asking about God's.

DANIEL: And the sharky machine intelligence is gonna move off-planet, expand out into the universe and leave the pets behind, living in shacks by rivers black with toxic sludge. We stare dumbly at the ruins of our cities in the red light of a dying sun. Our blind and twisted children play in the dirt. Might as well put them in a sack and drown them.

(DACK *and* DONNA *appear. Music. They sing, with a sharp dance routine.* JERZY *goes to* JULIETTE, *bows, asks her to dance. She hesitates, then gives in.* ABBY *approaches* DANIEL. KIMMIE *and* MARTY. *All dance during the following talk, with the occasional exception of the speaker.*)

MARTY: *(Sales talk)* Take it from Doctor Marty. I guarantee that in the future, you'll live forever.

KIMMIE: Forever?

MARTY: Close enough! Hundred eighty-five, maybe two hundred! New body parts, reconstructive surgery, beautiful drugs. Disease free! Hot and healthy! The golden years.

KIMMIE: You buy that? Sucker. Any happiness plan that depends on patching the body like a bald tire is for losers. Instead of separating from the body as you age, you get more connected to it. Meat is bound to disappoint you in the end. You're putting big money on a long shot and doubling up when you lose.

DANIEL: If I made—with my little nanoguys—a walking, talking, fuckable picture of you, would I need you? Don't answer that one. I'm busy working on a

combo of early Tuesday Weld and Combustible Annie
from high school....

KIMMIE: Want to be me? You send me a dollar
and a dime in a plain envelope and I send you the
access code for the neverending river of my sensory
experience and complete neurological correlates for
my physical and emotional responses. Been peeking
through the webcam at some sorority girl's low-res
bedroom antics? Here's the real thing and I give it to
you straight no chaser. All you do is plug in. If you
don't want to be me, access the archives—Hef's pool
party with the twins, or a moment of vision in the
Wind River Range--black crow flaps off that dead pine
tree, up into a cloudless sky.
Hey, darling, real life is just one more window.

(End music, end dance.)

DANIEL: You ever think, about your life I mean, that
you were given a job to do, a particular assignment,
and you're not doing it...

ABBY: *(Aside)* Every day...

DANIEL: In fact, sometimes you can't even remember
what the job is. You screwed up, and there's no way to
turn it around. Not anymore.

KIMMIE: Danny, you've been in Port Twilight too long.

JULIETTE: You didn't know what they were doing at the
lab. Not your fault.

DANIEL: My assistant. Invaluable.

MARTY: You knew. Underneath, you knew, and you
took their money anyway. Let it go. Now you're taking
my money.

KIMMIE: Hans and Fritz's money. From the Black
Forest. The elves give it to them to make movies.

JULIETTE: Daniel, you're a good person. I can tell.

MARTY: Is he? And am I a good person? Is Kimmie a good person?

JULIETTE: Yes. Yes you are. All of you.

MARTY: You're not the fastest little pony on the track, are you?

DANIEL: Marty, shut up.

JERZY: And me? Juliette, what about me? Am I a good person?

MARTY: Jerzy, stay outta this. (*To* DANIEL) Tell her to ease up on the goody-goody bullshit. Once we wrap she can come around, tell me how to live my life.

Uncomfortable silence, for a long moment.

JULIETTE: You know where I'd like to go? Home. My Mom's house in Minnesota. Snow on everything.

DANIEL: Won't help. This entire earth is inside some kinda plastic wrap, a clear film that seals in time. Everywhere else, they're living large in eternity, but we're in a little graveyard we made, stuck in a time flow that's not only slow, but a one way street, so rudimentary that even our chuckaluck brains can almost understand it. We call that dim grip consciousness. Its kindergarden. We have no idea what's actually happening. Not a clue.

18.

(*Night on the street outside the Clinic. From the curtained clinic window, a stream of light.* MOSHIACH *and the* SERVANT *wait for the* RABBI.)

SERVANT: Your appearance in this world gives me hope...hope for the future, and renewed faith in the Rabbi's wisdom.

(MOSHIACH's *voice is harsher and more guttural now.*)

MOSHIACH: The Rabbi is a fool. I was sent here by Lilith, who tried to tear out my tongue. I am her slave.

(Smoke begins to come from MOSHIACH's *mouth as he speaks. His torn tongue is green. He is revealed as a demon.)*

MOSHIACH: Without your opening of the gates, I could not have entered this world. So I will not kill you and eat you.

*(*MOSHIACH *grabs the* SERVANT's *arm, feels it.)*

MOSHIACH: Besides, you're too stringy to be tasty...

(The RABBI *emerges from the Clinic, and sees the revealed false* MOSHIACH. MOSHIACH *turns toward the* RABBI.)*

MOSHIACH: Sssssss! Tsssss!

RABBI: Aleph, Ham, Shem! Chachazit!

*(*MOSHIACH *laughs, and rips the* RABBI's *amulet from his neck, tossing it away.)*

MOSHIACH: Your religion is dead, and its holy names are useless jackal shit. All your lovers have forgotten you, old man. They seek you not. *(He laughs again, in his guttural way.)* There was a serious error in your incantations. I am a demon from Jeldred, the first world of darkness, set loose by you upon the earth. Here in Port Twilight I can kill and feed.

(The SERVANT *swings his shovel at* MOSHIACH. MOSHIACH *is quicker and stronger. He rips the shovel out of the* SERVANT's *hands, and smashes it into his head. The* SERVANT *goes down. His blood is everywhere.)*

(The false MOSHIACH *runs off, raving, the bloody shovel held high. The* RABBI *kneels down by the* SERVANT, *takes off his prayer shawl and uses it to staunch the bleeding from the* SERVANT's *head.)*

*(*DACK *and* DONNA *in another space.)*

DACK: You made a mistake, didn't you, Rabbi?

DONNA: And now your servant is bleeding his life away. Who will carry your whiskey and your shovel? Who will love your dying daughter, wrapped in the Tentacles, moaning in her pain and in her ecstasy?

RABBI: I wanted Moshiach to heal her. It was the reason I called him.

DACK: Selfish, wasn't it, Rabbi? To call for the Messiah, to bring the Last Judgment upon the world before its time, for the sake of one pathetic girl? But your sacred science opened the wrong door...

RABBI: SHUT UP! (*Looking down at the* SERVANT) He's dead.

(*In the distance, sound of the organ grinder's music. The* RABBI *stands, puts his bloody prayer shawl back on. He picks up his bottle of whiskey, takes a drink, walks slowly away...*)

19.

(*The group on the film set:* ABBY, DANIEL, JERZY, JULIETTE, KIMMIE *and* MARTY.)

(JERZY *patiently teaches* JULIETTE *to play a tune on the tin whistle. She's seated, blowing the whistle, trying the fingering. He's behind her, his face next to hers, hands reaching around to guide her hands on the instrument. At last she succeeds in playing a simple and beautiful melody.*)

JERZY: It's a white night. *Une nuit blanche.* A night of first love, the sea, the eyes of horses...

(*Soft music comes up under, quiet and somber—the Tyburn Jig, on the grave of the earth.*)

DANIEL: Go back a few hundred years and there is no "future" —tomorrow is the same as yesterday, or a century from now—pray, plow, sleep.

Now we have tomorrows that are damn sure to be different from today. So, we're the first humans to think about "the future," which is fucking ironic since we probably won't have one.

(ABBY *sits herself on* DANIEL'*s lap.*)

ABBY: On the other hand, mankind has lasted this long, even with his violent disposition, overwhelming stupidity, and bad manners.
Why don't you kiss me?

(DANIEL *does.*)

KIMMIE: *(looks at them, laughs)* George and Jane Jetson. The couple of the future.

ABBY: That's us, and we're A-O K. The scientists are at the wheel. We're in charge now, baby! Living large! We got genetically enhanced groceries, smart bombs, and the internet. Ten million channels and there's still nothing on. Who are we human beings? And what should we become? Who cares! We've given the pistol to a blind man in a lab coat, and he's walking down Main Street shooting at anything that moves.

DANIEL: Well said. Except that it's knee-jerk sixties hippy-dippy anti-science horseshit through and through. I can see damn well, and I'm trying to shoot what needs killing.

(MARTY *goes over to* ABBY *and* DANIEL.*)*

MARTY: I'm interested in this hi-tone dialogue, Danny boy, and I have some hard earned wisdom to contribute. There are only three great questions. I have searched for their answers throughout my life.

(MARTY *takes a long beat.* JULIETTE'*s curious.*)

JULIETTE: What questions?

DANIEL: Be careful. He's messing with you.

JULIETTE: Tell me. All three.

MARTY: One. What is it you have that I want? Two. What will it take for me to get it? Three. Once I've got it, what are the potential side effects?

KIMMIE: Marty, why in hell do you have to lo-ball the conversation here? You know better.

MARTY: Do I? Little dose of reality for my scientific consultants.

KIMMIE: Your reality, not mine.

(Silence for a long moment. JERZY *begins to play his tin whistle, mournful and slow.)*

JULIETTE: I'm fishing, on a dark lake, and I can't see the shore. There's mist, like I'm in a Chinese painting. Above me in the sky is a cloud panorama of the history of the earth—a king in his tower, dying soldiers, priests, a hunchback beggar, women weeping over half-formed children in the whiteness...till its all mercifully shredded by the wind. All this is above, and below I'm in my little drawing of a boat in a Chinese painting. A gentle tug on the line. Deep in the dark lake, a wonderful fish has taken my bait, hook and all.

KIMMIE: I'm getting a handle on this. You know what the future says, if we have one? No difference. Humans or intelligent machines, male or female, then or now, alive or dead, the dream or the waking. The differences slip away. And as our slick mental fingers, greased with a billion computations a millisecond, slide out into the galaxy we will leave our stinking bodies behind, and leave time behind us, and space. Our center will at last be everywhere, and our circumference nowhere. Hot damn.

*(*DACK *and* DONNA, *with an unseen band, begin to sing, softly continuing under...)*

KIMMIE: *(To* DANIEL*)* You never thought you'd roll another seven in this life. Did you?

ABBY: *(To* DANIEL*)* What is she talking about?

DANIEL: You.

MARTY: Last call!

KIMMIE: Drink up, sirs and ladies. Drink up!

Jerzy snaps his fingers in the air.

JERZY: HOLA! MUSIC!

(The music rises, tempo increasing, and becomes upbeat percussive.)

DANIEL: Put on your red dress, baby, and let's go dancing. After all, its the end of the world.

*(*DANIEL *is with* ABBY, MARTY *with* KIMMIE. JERZY *takes* JULIETTE *in his arms. The light changes, and the three couples dance on the air.)*

20.

(The Off Planet Message Exchange in the Ramona Hotel. The monitor staff of two are surrounded by empty beer cans, drug paraphernalia, half empty pizza boxes, audio equipment, headphones. The STATION CHIEF *addresses them.)*

STATION CHIEF: O P M E's mission, as I'm sure you recall, is to reveal and interpret the Intergalactic Tower of Babel. Our new decoding sequencer, installed last night, will make it audible and visible, a divine hand pulling back the red velvet curtain. The tower will appear—labyrinthine, seemingly impenetrable, the mental detritus and glory of a hundred thousand civilizations.

This decoding sequencer, sourced in the D N A of echolocating fruitbats, is a living and highly intelligent organism able to reprogram itself based on incoming frequencies.

I will now link it to our system.

(STATION CHIEF *throws a large switch. Strange hum as the new decoding device comes online. Then static, and a blur of languages, loud and harsh. On the giant screen, words and image fragments flash by too quickly to read. A screech, as of a needle skipping over a record, and the face of the Devil appears on the huge screen. He flicks his tongue. The devil morphs into Mister Softee, and then a standard* ALIEN, *gray in color, with large oval eyes in a noseless face. He's in mid-speech...*)

ALIEN: ...Assume your failure to respond indicates our first offer insufficient. I am now authorized to offer solutions to certain questions that have been perplexing your so-called scientists for some time. Is the Riemann hypothesis correct? What does the Poincare' conjecture imply for the existence of sub-atomic particles? Do other dimensions exist? Who lives there? We also offer definitive proof of the mass-gap hypothesis in quantum field theory, as well as ten thousand slaves of assorted species. All have been altered on the brothel moon for human satisfaction. In exchange, we want your entire planet, and we want it delivered vacant.

(*All the lights in the room go out, except on the screen. The* ALIEN *holds up his hands. He has six fingers on each, and at the tips of nine of his fingers a flame burns. The others light as the towns are recited.*)

ALIEN: Tssst. Paris. Tsssst! Hong Kong. Tssst, New York.

(*All twelve of the* ALIEN's *fingers are lit.*)

ALIEN: A man crouches in a cave. His brain burns in his skull. The Black Wind rises. And the face of the earth is without form and void...

(Static, and the image and audio of the ALIEN *begin breaking up. Chaos arrives in a loud and fragmented audio mix, with an accompanying visual mix onscreen.* MONITOR 1, MONITOR 2 *and the* STATION CHIEF *hide under the furniture, peek out. The mixes consists of:)*

(Audio: fragments of the Bible/ Shakespeare/ Proust/ Confucius/ Cervantes/ African languages/ Hebrew/ hisses, shrieks/ cries of babies/ wailing of the damned/ animal noises/ machine noises/ rocket take-offs/ futuristic T V shows [Star Trek, Jetsons, etc]. This material is chopped, spliced, loud, quiet, rhythmic, reversed, overlapping etc.)

(Visual: Towers of Babel/ images of nature/ human faces [childhood to old age, all races]/ rows of numbers flickering/ rows of letters [Cyrillic, Chinese, Arabic]/ Devil/ Alien/ Mr Softee/ religious symbols/ futuristic T V shows [Star Trek, Jetsons, Flash Gordon etc])/ rocketships/ constellations, star clusters, galaxies. This material is chopped, spliced, fragmented, tinted, overlapping, reversed, rhythmic, etc.)

(The chaos begins to fade, the screen dims. In the darkness, the STATION CHIEF *lights a candle. Out of the fading chaos, a child's voice emerges to chant alone...)*

CHILD'S VOICE:
Oranges and lemons
Say the bells of Saint Clements
When will you pay me?
Say the bells of Old Bailey
When I grow rich
Say the bells of Shoreditch
When will that be?
Say the bells of Stepney
I do not know
Says the great bell at Bow
Here comes a candle to light you to bed
Here comes a chopper to chop off your head

(Silence)

21.

(The row of SCIENTISTS, *faces and clothes covered with fine white ash. Scientist ghosts. They brush themselves off. Clouds of white ash fill the air. The hatrack still burns. One or two take off their dark glasses. They sing:)*

SCIENTISTS: *(Sing)*
Enjoy yourself, its later than you think

*(*SCIENTISTS *begin to dance as they sing. Science Dance Two.)*

SCIENTISTS: *(Still singing)*
Enjoy yourself, while you're still in the pink
The years go by as quickly as a wink
Enjoy yourself, enjoy yourself
Its later than you think.

(In the break between verses, extraordinary science dancing. It continues...)

SCIENTISTS: *(Still singing)*
Enjoy yourself, its later than you think
Enjoy yourself, while you're still in the pink
The years go by, as quickly as a wink
Enjoy yourself, enjoy yourself   Its later than you think.

(Big finish. End dance, end song.)

22.

*(*DACK *and* DONNA *appear. They hold torches.)*

DACK: Citizens of Port Twilight!

DONNA: All you pilgrims, traders, gamblers, whores!

DACK: Listen up!

*(*UNCLE NICK *appears.)*

UNCLE NICK: Five ninety-five, with fries.

DACK: Lock your doors! A demon rages through the streets of the city.

DONNA: He could be anywhere...the Palace Pier, the fan-tan parlors...

DACK: He'll leap from the shadows and rip out your throat.

DONNA: Stay out of back alleys.

(UNCLE NICK *checks* DONNA *out, smacks his lips, makes a vulgar gesture.*)

DONNA: Fuck off.

DACK & DONNA: *(With scary echo)* Beware! Beware! Beware!

(UNCLE NICK *fearfully scurries away, almost bumping into the* RABBI *who appears, walking slowly, bloody prayer shawl around his shoulders. He is lit by the torchlight.*)

RABBI: My loyal servant is dead. There is no one to carry the shovel and bury me where I fall. My daughter has lost her soul and no one can save her. The false Moshiach roams the city. I have brought a plague of blood. I do not want to think about it anymore. I am lost in the endless streets of Port Twilight, and not one of my students will leave the House of Study to help me. They sit by their smoking candles and stare at the Hebrew letters, with no idea what they can mean... Betrayed! A single prayer, spoken out of love and pity—it cannot be made good, not ever.

23.

(The room in the Port Twilight Clinic. From a distance, the music of MR ARGENTO.*)*

(The CLINICIAN *is fitting a new sheet to the bed. The old one, smeared with blood, lies on the floor nearby. In a corner*

of the room, SUZY *and* DIANA, *contemporary Riverdale High street clothes. The* CLINICIAN *finishes, turns to them.)*

CLINICIAN: A pleasure to see you again, Miss Johnson. It's always...

SUZY: Skip the fucking small talk. *(She walks toward the bed, stripping off her top. She kicks off her jeans, lies down on the bed on her back, looking up at the Tentacles.)* Just do it.

CLINICIAN: Your party.

(The CLINICIAN *sits at the computer. The Tentacles' lights brighten and pulse as it lowers.* SUZY's *body strains upward toward the machine, as if it were a descending lover.* DIANA *watches intently, her face expressionless, unreadable.)*

CLINICIAN: Welcome back to paradise.

(The shadow of the organ grinder appears at the window, his monkey Tomas on his shoulder. He turns the crank and the aria from "La Forza del Destino" rises, then fades as the room dims slowly to black, leaving only SUZY *visible, lit by the Tentacles attached to her body.)*

24.

(Darkness and silence at the Off Planet Message Exchange. One lit candle. The Station Chief, MONITOR 1, MONITOR 2 *and the* STATION CHIEF *still cower under furniture.)*

(An insistent beep begins. Suddenly the room's lights return. All three emerge. The STATION CHIEF *puts on a headset, hits a button. The beeping stops, and she listens.)*

STATION CHIEF: *(To caller)* O P M E Station Chief here... That's impossible. We've had contact. Explicit contact. Forty-seven seconds of the most... Yes, sir. I understand, but I don't feel we... Yes, sir. *(She hits a button, takes off her headset.)*

STATION CHIEF: We're closed. We've been shut down by Central. O P M E is kaputt.
They're scared. Some bullshit about sealing us off from intergalactic pollutants, mutant star spawn...
Whatever's going on out there, we're no longer listening.
You two get out of here.

MONITOR 2: What about you? What will...

STATION CHIEF: I intend to remain at the Off Planet Message Exchange until they come for me. I know they will.

(As the MONITORS *pick up their things, nod to the* STATION CHIEF, *and they're gone.)*

(The STATION CHIEF *begins to rips out wires, pull plugs, throw switches. As she does so, she whistles a little tune. "Enjoy yourself....")*

(Lights fade on the STATION CHIEF *as the monitoring station dies.)*

*(*MONITOR 1 *and* MONITOR 2 *seat themselves in rusted lawnchairs nearby.)*

DACK: Kaputt. Finished.

DONNA: So here we are—the Ramona Hotel down by the harbor, rusting lawn chairs, sound of the surf. On the window, the letters O P M E. Soon no one will remember what they stand for. Someone lights a cigarette...

DACK: *(Lighting a cigarette)* I need to find gainful employment.

DONNA: Don't remind me. We gotta live somehow. Well, we still got that movie gig, if they ever get it together...

DACK: I'm going to eat something at Big Wong's before we go back over there.

DONNA: You want company?

DACK: Yeah. I'd like that. You know, seems like you still love me...

DONNA: Let's go. I want some chop suey or something...

(DACK *and* DONNA *are gone.*)

25.

(The film set. MARTY *at a computer,* KIMMIE *and* JERZY. DANIEL *is with* ABBY *and* JULIETTE.*)*

KIMMIE: *(Holding a drink)* It's late, isn't it? Tail end of a white night... Drink up.

*(*KIMMIE *does. So does* DANIEL. MARTY *types.)*

MARTY: I'll write the fucker myself—boy meets girl, boy loses girl etcetera. Everything shiny and sexy. In the future. Years from now. When we're all dead and sleeping in our graves. Main thing is I can write it in two days and shoot it in two weeks. Same set. *(He keeps typing.)*

DANIEL: Most people don't make it through to any kind of happiness—too many detours. Self-indulgence, illness, laziness...

ABBY: Stupidity.

JULIETTE: Alcohol.

DANIEL: Fear. Just stay in the shallow end, son, water's so warm its like wading in your own piss. And you'll never drown. *(To* ABBY*)* You know what, Professor? I'm gonna be a mountain man, the Brooks Range in Alaska. No cellphone, no lab equipment, no books, five days to get to a road. That's in good weather. In summer.

ABBY: Wimpy man like you, you'll never make it up there.

DANIEL: Won't I?

ABBY: You'll go nuts the first winter. Unless you pack in a portable generator and love talking to yourself.

DANIEL: I'm just bringing a knife, good boots, and...

ABBY: A bear will eat you. You'll be dead before the first snow.

DANIEL: You're not making this easy...

JULIETTE: You shouldn't drink so much.

ABBY: That is obvious, to everyone except...

DANIEL: Both of you are self-righteous assholes. *(He stands, takes another drink, staggers for a moment.)*

DANIEL: What I've been trying to do, Abby, is invite you.

ABBY: Invite me?

DANIEL: To the mountains. Brooks Range.

(DANIEL stumbles, falls to the floor, and lies there. DACK and DONNA appear.)

DACK: And once again, Juliette kneels down by him, shakes him gently...

(JULIETTE kneels down by DANIEL. She shakes him gently...)

JULIETTE: Wake up. Wake up, dammit!

(The phone begins ringing.)

DONNA: And once again, the ringing of the phone, harsh, insistent.

(KIMMIE picks it up.)

KIMMIE: Marty Schott Productions. *(Listens)* Danny!

(KIMMIE, carrying the phone, goes over to DANIEL. She kicks him, not too hard, in the side. He manages to roll over.)

KIMMIE: It's for you, Doctor Milton.

(KIMMIE *holds out the phone.* DANIEL *struggles to a standing position, takes it.*)

DANIEL: *(Into phone)* Yeah. *(Listens)* Yes, it's me.

(*As* DANIEL*'s listening to the call...*)

DACK: The phone call, and then the Lincoln Towncar, the familiar streets of Port Twilight, the movie set, the stories, and dawn about to...

DANIEL: O K. O K. Yeah, I'll get back to you. *(He hangs up the phone.)*

DANIEL: My boss at the lab. Seems they have copies of all the genetic material I took. Hundreds of them. They were also monitoring my computer. They've got backups of every file I trashed.
And the fuckers want me back.

(*Lights brighten on* MARTY, *typing the new script.*)

MARTY: Camera crew's gonna arrive in... *(Checks watch)* ...three hours. They're gonna need the first five setups, at least...
Abby!

(*ABBY goes over to* MARTY.)

MARTY: Honey, you're fired.

ABBY: You should have fired me weeks ago. Good luck, Marty. Make something decent out of this mess.

MARTY: Yeah, sure.

(*ABBY goes to* DANIEL. *He's shaky, and she gets his arm around her shoulder.*)

ABBY: You need some air. Should be almost dawn...

(*ABBY and* DANIEL *walk off together, slowly. They're gone.* JERZY *begins to play his tin whistle...*)

(*KIMMIE goes over to* MARTY.)

KIMMIE: It's cooled off a bit. Little breeze off the ocean... How's the script coming?

MARTY: It's no work of genius, but it's getting there... You know, I always thought, what's a girl like you doing with a jerk like me? And then I always thought, hey, if I keep on making money, maybe she won't leave.

KIMMIE: That's not it, Marty. Never was. Not even for a moment. You are a jerk, you know. For even thinking that shit.

MARTY: You don't want to be in this one, do you?

KIMMIE: I never wanted to be in any of them.

MARTY: Donna can do your role. We'll find another kid to...

KIMMIE: That's the easy part. We still got a crew coming in at eight. We gotta pay them. You gotta give them something to shoot...
You know something, Marty? We're born, we live awhile, and the worm gets us all. That's it, you know. I saw it on a sundial once—I even remember the Latin. "Umbrae umbrarum vitu soluimus." Shadows we are, and like shadows we depart. This life has no meaning but what we poor creatures give it. And that's just local, Marty. The space between the stars is absolute, with no beginning and no end. Nothing we make can ever fill it.
Write a good one, baby. Put in a joke or two. Let 'em laugh in the dark, and let the boy get the girl.

(MARTY *begins again to type.* JERZY *continues to play.* KIMMIE *drinks.* DACK *and* DONNA *off to one side. Music.* JERZY *puts away his tin whistle and he and* JULIETTE *dance again, this time a slow one. The music is quiet, almost unheard.)*

(Suddenly, a flash of white light, the same as hit the row of scientists, hits the film set. All freeze for a split second, then continue as before. The slightest trace of white ash falls from above. The music ends.)

JERZY: I need to get something to eat, chop suey, maybe. There's a place over on the boulevard. Big Wong's.

JULIETTE: They have coffee?

JERZY: Yeah. They have coffee.

JULIETTE: Good. That's good.

JERZY: What is it you have that I want?

JULIETTE: And what will it take for me to get it?

JERZY: I love you, you know. We can marry, make babies that look like you, like tiny...

JULIETTE: Let's start by getting coffee.

JERZY: O K. I can wait. Soon, beyond Port Twilight, we will take delight in the shining world. You and me.

JULIETTE: Let's go.

(JERZY and JULIETTE go.)

(MARTY still types, KIMMIE alongside him. In an upstage corner of the warehouse, almost invisible, an old Chinese woman sits silently. She tucks fortunes into cookies, one by one.)

(The spaceship set lights up. Within it, MR CHANG, asleep at the desk of the Port Twilight Motel. He wakes from his dream for just a moment...)

MR CHANG: Too much talking! Quiet, or I kick you all out... *(He goes back to sleep...)*

(Darkness)

26.

(DANIEL *alone.*)

DANIEL: I remember the Ramona Hotel, and the
waxwork of the three fates out on the pier, and Tomas
the monkey in his red coat, tin cup full of fortunes, and
a Polish gypsy with his dancing bear, and who knows
what wood in the Carpathians the bear was caught
in, and who cares that his mother wanders the forest
searching for him, and clambers down a hillside into
a village and shuffles along Main Street, heavy head
swinging side to side until the bullet hits her behind
the ear and she falls to the ground. The dark hole wells
with blood, soaking her fur.

*(The organ grinder and his monkey appear in the distance.
He begins to play.)*

DANIEL: And there was a holy man and his daughter,
and a scientist, and a trained lamb that walked up
Jacob's ladder. All gone now, all gone into the mist,
and soon everyone who remembers them and weeps at
their passing will be gone as well, into the mist, never
to return.

27.

*(DACK and DONNA as they were in the beginning, DACK at
his desk, and DONNA at her full-length mirror. The RABBI
appears, walking slowly. The organ grinder continues to
play.)*

DONNA: The boulevard, at this hour of night, is nearly
empty, as everyone already knows. The Rabbi wanders
under the violet streetlamps. A woman walks past
him, and her high heels click on the pavement. Is that
Juliette, or is it Veronica? She disappears in the shadow
of the giant cypress trees.

Soon, once again, the Rabbi will reach the White River, and look down into the flowing water.

(The RABBI *is gone. The organ grinder is gone.)*

DACK: And the scientists are dusted with a fine white ash, the false Moshiach rises from the river, Port Twilight is created, and the Tower of Babel falls—all happening once again for an audience dreaming of their after theatre pleasures—dinner, love, sleep.
The end of words, the end of the world. That's all, folks. That's all there is to say, in this body, in this time, all there is, there ain't no more.

28.

(The row of SCIENTISTS *appears one final time. The hatrack is as it was in the beginning. Their faces and clothing are still marked with white ash. One tosses his fedora skyward. One weeps. One* SCIENTIST *checks his watch. One by one, all turn to stare out at the horizon. A distant siren...)*

END PLAY